Walker Art Center

ART SPACES

Cathy Madison

SCALA

more than a museum

More than 125 years ago, a Minneapolis man built a room onto his house, mounted his 20 favorite paintings on the walls, and opened his door to everyone who wanted to come in. In 1879, Thomas Barlow (T. B.) Walker's art gallery was a unique venue for the arts of its time. It was also a modest start for a contemporary arts center now revered throughout the world for the range and vitality of its visual arts, performing arts, and media arts programs. Today the Walker Art Center ranks among the ten most-visited art museums in the United States and, together with the adjacent Minneapolis Sculpture Garden, attracts nearly one million visitors a year.

Yet the Walker is not prototypical; "museum" has always been too narrow a concept to encompass its mission. Rather than merely providing a place for people to see art, the Walker is a catalyst for the creative expression of artists and the active engagement of audiences. In pursuing those goals, its stewards have long encouraged expansion and innovation not only in exhibitions, programs, and art forms, but also in the buildings that house them.

T. B. Walker nurtured a populist, if not always popular, view of art and its value in society. Unfettered by the more staid museum traditions of his fellow city fathers, the Walker's progressive, eclectic founder followed his own muse in the art he chose to collect and also in how he shared it. It is only fitting that what began as an uncommon plush and gilt-frame gallery in his home has endured, and indeed thrived upon adventurous structural evolutions.

As art has come and gone at the Walker, so too have its walls. Moderne replaced minarets, only to be succeeded by loftlike minimalism, now transformed through glass and steel into a structure that marries inside to outside, city bustle to park tranquility, and painting to performance in a way that is as interactive as today's digital

>
Installation view of the exhibition *Walk Around Time: Selections from the Permanent Collection*, 2003

world. Despite its location on a somewhat cramped site close to the city center, the Walker has managed to adapt itself physically to conceptual changes in the art world and in society as a whole.

<
Walker Director
Kathy Halbreich, 2004

This, according to Director Kathy Halbreich, is as it should be. "The Walker Art Center has an unparalleled commitment to fostering new ways of thinking about, learning from, and experiencing the contemporary arts for diverse audiences," she says. "Equally fundamental is our dedication to offering artists the opportunity to make new work that reveals the questions that shape us as individuals, communities, and cultures."

homegrown beginning

>
T. B. Walker,
circa 1890

Small and wiry with blue eyes and close-cropped beard, T. B. Walker was a stubborn man of strong opinions who refused to eat grapefruit and slept with a pistol under his pillow. As bold and straightforward as the art the Walker now displays, he knew what he wanted and usually got it. While staunchly loyal to his Minneapolis home and the civic promise it represented, he was also a pioneer, constantly pushing toward new horizons.

Born in Xenia, Ohio, in 1840, he got his first job cutting biscuits in a bakery in 1849, the year his father died of cholera while crossing the plains to join the Gold Rush. As an enterprising teen, he made a small purchase—a job lot of two-dollar trees, from which he fashioned clocks, butter bowls, and railroad ties to peddle—that foreshadowed his future as a lumber baron. It was his budding career as a traveling grindstone salesman, however, that led him to Minneapolis.

At MacGregor's Landing in Iowa on a perfect summer day in 1862, he paused to schmooze with a stranger named Robinson. Bristling with enthusiasm, the fellow confided that a booming river town up north was a great place for a young man to make a good living. In fact, he added, the *Diamond Joe* steamboat tied to the dock would be departing for Minneapolis within the hour. The whistle blew. On a whim, the fearless peddler grabbed his grindstones and hopped aboard. It must have been his day; upon disembarking, he met a 24-year-old lad named Jim who also was destined for an important role in Minnesota history. Railroad king James J. Hill became a lifelong friend.

<
Residence and gallery of Thomas Barlow Walker, 803 Hennepin Avenue, Minneapolis, circa 1900

appointed mathematics professor at a Wisconsin university. He got the job, but "Indian trouble" held up the mail for months. By the time the letter arrived, he was surveying government land and laying groundwork for a new venture. His Red River Lumber Company became the nation's third largest, providing riches that by 1923 placed T. B. among the world's 10 wealthiest men. His logging camps became towns; Walker, in northern Minnesota, bears his name.

He married Harriet Granger Hulet in 1863, and together they had six sons and two daughters. A decade later, they bought the home that would become the Walker Art Gallery's first site: 803 Hennepin Avenue, between Eighth and Ninth streets in the heart of downtown, where the State Theatre now stands. Early accounts dubbed it the first unfenced lot in Minneapolis; T. B. was roundly criticized for its probable ruination by cows, chickens, and frolicking children.

It was 1874—coincidentally, the same year that the Lowry Mansion, the Walker family's future home and current Walker Art Center site, was built. T. B. and his wife set off for New York City to buy furnishings, including art that their daughter, Julia, had requested to decorate her bedroom walls. She was only nine, but Dad complied.

His first purchase was a portrait of a monk by Italian artist Tambourine.

"I began collecting paintings, engravings, and chromos as you would illustrated books—something to look at or to read; something to pass on to the next person," he explained, according to biographer Clara Nelson. His criteria was basic; of the paintings he sought and examined, he bought "only modern pictures that came within my means and that appeared to be of sufficient importance and value to make this purchase worthwhile."

He allegedly acquired his first "old master"—Rembrandt Peale's *Portrait of George Washington*—as payment of a bad debt; other acquisitions included still lifes by C. P. Reams, a George Romney portrait, and a George Inness landscape. By 1879, he was ready to invite people into the 16-by-30-foot Walker Art Gallery, built between his residence and carriage house. It wasn't fancy, but it was conveniently located on the streetcar line. Initially, a card was required to enter, but soon the door was opened to anyone who rang the bell. Visitors would deposit their parasols in a container, then be taken on tours and allowed to wander.

T. B.'s penchant for engaging the general public extended beyond sharing art and feeding any tramps who came to the door. Eschewing fiction but believing that everyone should have access to books, he quietly bought enough (more than 70) memberships in the Athenaeum, a private book club, to achieve a controlling interest. So began the Minneapolis Public Library; he remained president for 44 years until his death.

A second maid was hired to handle the crowds at what turned out to be the first public art gallery west of the

^
The galleries in T. B. Walker's home, circa 1904

Mississippi River. Eight additions were built between 1887 and 1913; the first, 19-by-30 feet, cost $2,000, and the last, 40-by-100 feet, cost $5,000. By 1915, the 14-room structure attracted 100,000 visitors annually, and by the 1920s, the Walker Art Gallery—containing 400 paintings and other objects—nearly filled a city block.

In 1912, a visitor described the experience:

■ A few days ago two of us availed ourselves of the opportunity so freely offered, and rang the bell at the great, rambling, unpretentious-looking residence of Mr. Walker. A pleasant-faced maid opened the door and ushered us into a series of handsome rooms devoted to the art treasures, where a few other visitors were already enjoying the collection. Most exquisitely furnished are the different rooms, elegantly carved chairs and tables of rare woods being scattered through them. The handsome carpets are almost covered by rare Oriental rugs. These latter form a fascinating and almost priceless collection by themselves, and some evident connoisseurs were indulging in subdued exclamations of ecstasy as they bent over one and another. But the walls of this gallery! Almost every available inch was covered by the rarest of pictures! ■

^
T. B. Walker purchased this eighteenth-century Chinese jade mountain in 1912 for $4,000.

<
Vases and paintings in T. B. Walker's art gallery, 1909

In fact, T. B.'s tastes in art had expanded along with his gallery. Having long been uninterested in those "little clay pots" (about which he grumbled to New York pals Henry Clay Frick and J. Pierpont Morgan), he reconsidered and began buying Chinese porcelain. He also collected seventeenth-, eighteenth-, and nineteenth-century jade, amassing one of the most complete collections in the country. The gallery was about to burst its seams.

art's home on the hill

It wasn't a need for art space that prompted the family to move their gallery to a subdivision; it was Harriet, who decried Hennepin Avenue's increasing hustle and bustle. In 1916, the Walkers bought the 3.5-acre Lowry homestead at Two Groveland Terrace, on a hill overlooking the city center. Sadly, Harriet died in 1917 while on yet another New York home-furnishing trip, before she could enjoy the elegant mansion and its relative quietude.

T. B., nearing 80, began thinking seriously about his legacy. In 1918 he made a formal offer, via the library board, to deed part of the Lowry property to the city to be used for a library and attached museum. He would throw in, as a gift, his art collection; newspaper accounts claimed it was worth nearly $5 million, although city fathers disputed such a lofty valuation. One egotistical detail stuck in their craw: he wanted to call his venture Walker Terrace.

His intentions were grand. "Books and art will be joined hand in hand for the use of the people," he said. "The view from the building will be remarkable, and the center will be among the most magnificent in America." Although the Minnesota legislature authorized the sale of $500,000 in bonds, only half of them sold, and the deal languished.

Controversy reigned. Arguably an outsider in local art circles, T. B. bristled when the Minneapolis Institute of Arts, backed by the Business Men's Association, reiterated an earlier offer to house his artworks in a special Walker wing. The Institute was too far from "the coming civic center" of the city, as he saw his beloved Lowry Hill, and he would not allow his collection "to be tucked away in some isolate room."

>
The Walker Art Galleries, 1930

In 1923, disgusted with the dearth of cooperation, he rescinded his offer and took back his land. "My personal property . . . has not been suitably cared for by you, nor cared for at all," he wrote. Like the fabled Little Red Hen, he would do the work himself, though in this case, the community would reap the benefits of his efforts. In 1925, construction began on a two-story structure at 1710 Lyndale Avenue South, where the Walker Art Center still stands.

Designed by Olaf Thorshov of Long & Thorshov, Minneapolis, and built by the James Leck Construction Company, the Venetian-style building was as grand as its owner's intentions. The quasi-Moorish facade, made of stone, terra-cotta, and brick, was replete with pilasters, minarets, and arched French windows. Inside, the 34-by-45-foot vestibule boasted fluted columns and terrazzo floors. Reviewers admired the "Neoclassical conventions" of the grand staircase and symmetrical plan. The $300,000 building housing the galleries, one reviewer wrote, reflected the "Romantic revival spirit of American architecture of the '20s. . . . Romanesque colonnettes of the facade

<
T. B. Walker in the newly completed Walker Art Galleries building, 1927

>
Walker Art Galleries, circa 1930

>>
Painting galleries, Walker Art Galleries, circa 1930

reflected the pleasure palaces of Venice and Isfahan." The founder could not have asked for a better face for his 31 galleries of archaeological and anthropological artifacts, decorative arts, American Indian portraits, and Oriental objects, not to mention his traditional European and American paintings.

The Walker Art Galleries opened to the public on May 22, 1927. Five thousand people came that first day to view some 3,500 objects and paintings, which art critic John K. Sherman would later call "a musty mixture where masterworks jostled their poor relations." Such a review probably would not have bothered Thomas Barlow Walker; eclecticism defined him. When he died on July 28, 1928, at age 88, leaving an estate worth $1.62 million and an art collection worth an additional $100 million, he had accomplished his dream: "I had a feeling of good will toward the people of Minneapolis particularly, and it was my desire to live here all my life and to do all possible toward the upbuilding of the prosperity of the community."

new name, new face

>
Director Daniel Defenbacher (center) quizzes panelists during an "Inquisition" in the Walker Art Center lobby, March 1940

The Depression, not surprisingly, was hard on the Walker Art Galleries. Staff shrank to three: T. B.'s former chauffeur, a maintenance man, and self-trained curator R. (Rueben) Adams, who had helped the family with land, insurance, and tax matters since 1904. Hudson Walker, a grandson and New York City gallery owner who served as president of the American Artists Foundation, took over when Adams died in 1935. He passed the torch to his sister, Louise Walker McCannel, in 1937.

By 1939, combined efforts of the newly formed Minnesota Arts Council and the Work Projects Administration (WPA) revived the Walker legacy. The WPA offered to pay a staff of 30 to develop a civic art center, the largest of the 50 that so far had been established across the country (there would eventually be 73). As T. B. himself might have envisioned, proposed activities, including free lectures, workshops, and performances, had to be accessible to everyone in accordance with federal mandate.

The family-run T. B. Walker Foundation granted temporary financial and operational control of the Walker Art Galleries to Daniel Defenbacher, who had been directing the WPA staff. Free use of the building and access to the permanent collection was contingent upon the Minnesota Arts Council raising $5,500. An 80-year-old Minneapolis violin maker, A. T. Weston, made the first contribution. "I don't know how I could spend $50 better," he said.

On the bitter cold night of January 4, 1940, a huge crowd attended the reopening of the newly named Walker Art Center. A few years later, in a prescient statement given the design focus of the Walker's current building, Defenbacher elaborated on the name: "An Art Center is a 'town meeting' in a field of human endeavor as old as man himself. By definition, it is a meeting place for all the arts. It provides space in which the public can both participate and be a spectator."

^
The Spring Dance Festival, organized by Gertrude Lippincott, was the first performance held at the Walker Art Center, June 1940.

^
^
Walker Art Center reception and book corner entrance, circa 1946

^
Evelyn Raymond's sculpture class at the Walker Art Center, 1947

The early 1940s marked the Walker's first performing arts event and the launch of a bookstore and an art school that trained a thousand students a year until it closed in 1950. During the decade, many original holdings, from paintings to pottery, were sold. Acquired in their stead were such works as Lyonel Feininger's *Church of the Minorites II* (1926) and Edward Hopper's *Office at Night* (1940).

>
Edward Hopper
Office at Night (1940)
oil on canvas
Gift of the T. B. Walker Foundation, Gilbert M. Walker Fund, 1948

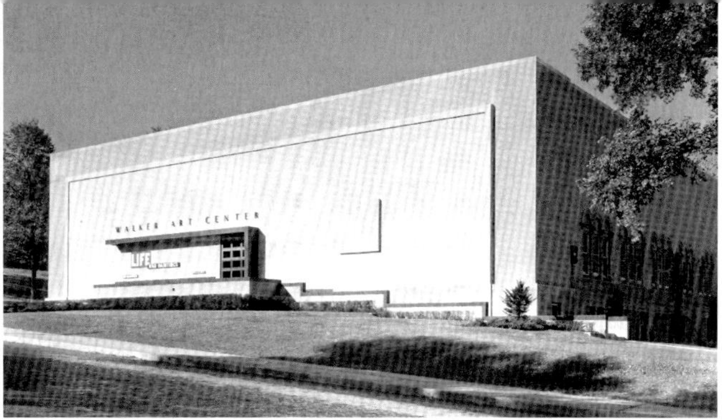

City Gets Famous Blue Horses Hitler Rejected

Masterpiece by Franz Marc Purchased by Walker Gallery

Hey, Adolf—Minneapolis has those Blue Horses you didn't like.

Remember? "Blue Horses" by Franz Marc, which art critics now consider one of the masterpieces of Twentieth century painting.

You, Adolf, got that picture heaved out of Germany because you thought that little paper-hanging job you had in Vienna made you an art critic. But the real critics have got you pegged as an artist just like the Russians have got you pegged as a soldier.

Either way it spells BUM.

You didn't like "Blue Horses," the big massive oil showing three champing horses in blue against a landscape of bright red hills. It was a little too modernistic for you (particularly because the horses are blue rather than white, brown or black) so you just labeled it "degenerate" and kicked it out of the Reich.

But now the critics are calling Franz Marc the Matisse of Germany and Alfred Barr, director of the Museum of Modern Art, says Marc was the most brilliant of twentieth century German painters.

Marc's famous painting hangs today in Walker Art Center, the latest acquisition of the Minneapolis gallery purchased through the Gilbert M. Walker Memorial fund. The picture is the first example of modern art to be presented in the gallery's collections. Officers say it marks another step toward carrying out the policy of developing a comprehensive collection for [illegible] tional purposes, while at the same time maintaining a high artistic standard.

So Hitler's boner becomes Minneapolis' gain.

IT'S A MASTERPIECE, BUT HITLER WOUDN'T KNOW IT.

As the art metamorphosed, so did the building. In late spring 1944, frost and rain sent a large chunk of terra-cotta crashing down in front of the main entrance, narrowly missing a group of schoolchildren. Minneapolis architects Magney, Tusler, and Setter were charged with the facade's remodel, which they completed by fall. Rebuilt with Mankato stone and Cold Spring granite, the moderne facade was all smooth surface and straight lines—a dramatic shift from Moorish minarets, and not universally loved. "Public opinion is divided on its attractiveness, and people who don't care for functional broad-planed architecture still compare it to a gas station" (*Minneapolis Tribune*).

Yet the changes matched those on the inside, where it was the versatility, not individual pieces or exhibitions, that garnered public enthusiasm and cooperation. Some acquisitions were controversial, such as Franz Marc's 1911 *Die grossen blauen Pferde* (*The Large Blue Horses*), which Hitler had declared "degenerate" because "there are no blue horses." This oil painting, purchased in 1942, was the Walker's first modern-art acquisition.

Controversy and the Walker would prove congenial mates. "Art is a lively subject at the Walker Art Center. It is . . . psychologically based in an approach that is essentially youthful, experimental, modern-minded. Tradition has no home behind the severe, streamlined facade of the gallery on the Lyndale-Hennepin hill. The last vestiges of highnose aloofness are gone" (*Minneapolis Tribune*).

<<
The Walker Art Center's moderne facade, 1944

^
Newspaper report on the Walker's newest acquisition

>
Franz Marc
Die grossen blauen Pferde (1911)
oil on canvas
Gift of the T. B. Walker Foundation, Gilbert M. Walker Fund, 1942

everyday art place

<
The Everyday Art Gallery featured changing exhibitions of modern design and architecture

>
Idea House I under construction, 1941

Accessibility, T. B. Walker's mantra, continued to define the Walker's focus. Its art must be helpful and useful to as many people as it can wisely reach, its leaders vowed. A tribute to this belief was the opening in 1946 of the Everyday Art Gallery, one of the first permanent gallery spaces devoted to design in a U.S. museum. The *Everyday Art Quarterly: A Guide to Well-Designed Products* (later renamed *Design Quarterly*), the first U.S. museum journal on design, was launched six months later.

Useful art included Idea House I, the first full-scale exhibition house created by an art museum. Built in 1941 for $6,954.07 plus in-kind donations from 40 local manufacturers and merchants, the wood structure boasted unusual features: five multiuse rooms with movable walls, a second-story porch, large back windows, and a lower level only partially below ground.

Critics scoffed at what they considered "excessive" costs for the average buyer, but average buyers flocked to see rooms painted French blue, Chinese red, chartreuse, and beige. More people visited Idea House I than any other exhibition in Walker history to that date: 36,842 people paid a dime, and 183 managed to sneak in free. It proved so popular that Idea House II was built in 1947 on the museum's grounds at 1719 Bryant Avenue South.

^
Exterior view of Idea House II, 1947

>
Idea House II living room, 1947

While Idea House II attracted fewer visitors, it garnered greater national attention for its prescient glimpse of what would become a dominant housing style, the split-level ranch, complete with innovative furniture and modern appliances. The design so intrigued *Life* magazine that it selected a family of four to live in the house for a week and record their reactions—a precursor of today's reality shows in print.

^
Director H. H. Arnason (left) at the Center Arts Council Ball, May 1954

>
Walker Art Galleries, Sculpture Court, circa 1963

Director H. Harvard Arnason, who wrote *The History of Modern Art* and chaired the University of Minnesota's Art Department, took the Walker helm in 1951; his many contributions reflected his commitments to modernism and academia. He launched the Center Arts Council, which began hosting performing arts and film presentations in 1953. Screenings showcased Hollywood luminaries such as Alfred Hitchcock and Billy Wilder as well as foreign directors. Arnason focused on acquiring additional modern works, especially sculpture, and organizing large-scale surveys and solo-artist exhibitions.

^
From left: Design Curator Mildred Friedman, Director Martin Friedman, and Vice-President Hubert H. Humphrey, 1967

His successor, Martin Friedman, named director in 1961, pushed even further into the contemporary zone, acquiring such works as Chuck Close's *Big Self-Portrait* (1967–68), mounting ambitious world-touring exhibitions, and championing more experimental art forms. The Walker launched two public film series, hosted its first artist-in-residence, and welcomed dancers such as Merce Cunningham and Twyla Tharp. It also brought popular musicians to town, including Arlo Guthrie, B. B. King, Led Zeppelin, and the Steve Miller Band.

>
Director Martin Friedman (left) and Marcel Duchamp (center) during an interview at the Walker, 1965

<
Chuck Close with *Big Self-Portrait* (1967–68), installed in the Walker exhibition *Close Portraits*, 1980

^
The Guthrie Theater, 1963

A museum-building frenzy ensued during that decade, which Friedman called the "art-a-go-go" period. Twenty-six percent of the 340 U.S. art museums that existed in 1978 were built between 1960 and 1969. Although not completed until 1971, the new Walker was one of them.

In 1961, Idea House I was torn down to make room for the Guthrie Theater; the T. B. Walker Foundation provided the site and yearly maintenance, and contributed $500,000 toward construction. Ralph Rapson designed the fanciful building, which opened May 7, 1963, when 1,400 people attended a production of *Hamlet*.

For the Walker itself, it was the best of times — the *New York Times* called it "this country's most vigorous outpost of in-art" — and the worst of times. Its 1927 building was in sad shape — sinking, in fact. According to one source, its site was originally "a canyon so deep that the tree tops did not reach street level." By 1962, the building's northwest corner had sunk 13 inches into the marshy bog; New York architect Edward Larrabee Barnes was hired to correct the foundation problems.

In 1967, 327,000 people — more than twice as many as a decade earlier — visited the Walker. But conditions were less than ideal. The Walker needed new, flexible spaces for its artists and the changing nature of the artwork in its exhibitions. The Guthrie's threshold butted up against the Walker's loading dock, so the two attractions had no common entrance.

V
Partygoers have one last fling in the Walker building before demolition begins, March 1969

>
Demolition of the Walker Art Center building, March 1969

In 1968, both institutions considered relocating to Nicollet Island, Gateway Center, or northeast Loring Park. But they decided to stay put, turning their attention instead to fund-raising; they needed $6.2 million, $4.5 million of which would be used to raze the moderne building and erect the new Walker. The T. B. Walker Foundation donated more than $1 million, 20 corporations gave $2.5 million, and six families each donated $100,000 or more. The smallest gift came from a frail, elderly man who entered the Walker bookstore one day in January 1969 and made his way over to the clerk. He put seven cents in her hand. It was all he could spare, he said, but he wanted to participate.

art center expands

On March 7, 1969, after a raucous March 1 closing event at which partygoers were encouraged to draw on the walls, the wrecking ball struck. While "Museum without Walls" exhibitions and activities continued off-site — the Performing Arts Department, destined to become the nation's largest museum-based program, was officially formed in 1970, and in 1971 the Education Department was expanded to include community outreach — the new Walker Art Center became a new challenge for the architect.

Edward Larrabee Barnes had done master plans and buildings at several institutions, including Yale, the University of Chicago, and Bennington College, but he had never before tackled a museum. Perceiving the Walker's position in the art world as "somewhere to the left of SoHo," he risked dispensing with the architect's tradition of using structure to make a strong expressive statement and instead designed a minimalist building that would showcase the art.

"A museum is not a temple to the donors, or a monument to the architect, or a security vault — in short, it is not a thing in itself. It is part of the fabric of daily life, sharing urban benefits and problems with its neighbors," Barnes wrote after completing the building.

He paid close attention to the essentials: room proportions, quality of light, and the way people moved through the spaces. Flow was more important than form, he believed, noting two kinds of public circulation: classic (direct movement to individual galleries surrounding a central stairwell), and Guggenheim-like sequential, where visitors progressed in a programmed order.

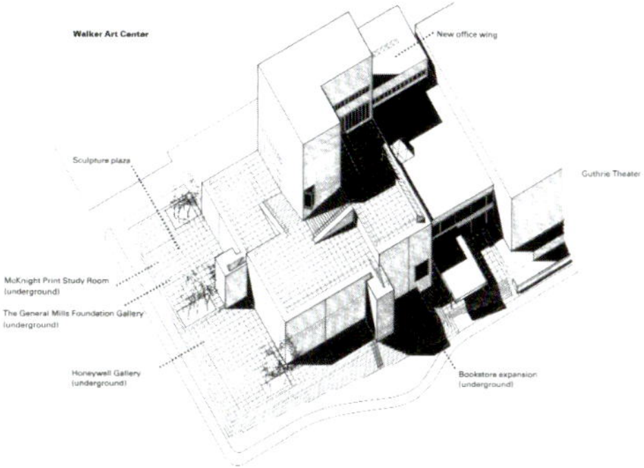

<
Schematic of Edward Larrabee Barnes' Walker Art Center building

v
View of the downtown Minneapolis skyline from the terraces of the Barnes building, circa 1972

Barnes used both in his plan. Like a rectangular helix, seven boxlike galleries radiated from a central core that contained the elevator and stairs. Size varied; one was 48-by-67 feet, another 56-by-82 feet with a 17.5-foot ceiling. Atop the galleries were three innovative outdoor sculpture terraces, dubbed "pedestals" by Barnes, that would showcase sculpture by such artists as Sol LeWitt, Claes Oldenburg, and Alexander Calder. From these vantage points, T. B. Walker might have waxed eloquent about the views overlooking the city center he held so dear.

The exterior of the new Walker was not granite, as originally planned, but plum-colored brick. The configuration of these huge, brownish blocks prompted one critic to suggest that the building could "easily be mistaken for an elegant warehouse." But with simplicity and reserve, elegant proportions and sensitivity to materials, Barnes effectively counterbalanced the light, open airiness of the Guthrie. The Walker was solid and inward, supportive of the expansive art within.

■ The Center is cubist, the way it piles up blocks of space. It does resemble Carcassone, the ramparted-fortress city in southern France, in its solidity and the way it suggests it will last secure. But, one trusts, the Center will be an art citadel without adopting a siege mentality. The special merit of the Walker lately has been the way it has not hidden behind, or let itself be trapped by walls (*Minneapolis Star*). ■

^
Walker Art Center building and entry, 1971

>
Walker Art Center building, 1971

EXIT

<
Walker Art Center galleries, 1971

>
Walker Art Center galleries, 1971

V
The Walker Art Center/Guthrie Theater complex, 1971

Inside the galleries, all was white and spare. Floors were white terrazzo. Walls were few; the use of precast concrete T-sections produced column-free spaces with uninterrupted vistas. Traditional galleries offered visitors a safe haven for dealing with the past, one reviewer noted, but here it was more important to create the right environment for the experimentation and creation that is contemporary art. According to the *Star Tribune*, "It has an unadorned interior—painted concrete ceilings, no moldings, cornices, or door frames—that perfectly complements today's often aggressively intellectual art."

The entrance moved from Lyndale Avenue to Vineland Place, where the Walker could share a large, welcoming lobby with the Guthrie. A 350-seat auditorium was installed, and gallery space increased by 50 percent in a building that now encompassed 82,000 square feet.

^
Lynda Benglis' wall piece created for the opening exhibition in the new building, 1971

<
Sam Gilliam's lobby installation of painted cloth created for the opening exhibition in the new building, 1971

Four thousand people, including Minnesota Governor Wendell Anderson and three generations of Walkers, attended the opening on May 15, 1971. Compared to the 3,500 objects and paintings celebrated at the 1927 opening, the current permanent collection was modest: 400 paintings and 130 sculptures. But *Works for New Spaces*, an opening exhibition that featured some 20 large-scale pieces commissioned by the Walker and displayed in three of seven galleries, on the roof terraces, and in nearby parks, spoke volumes about the focus on contemporary and site-specific works.

Along a 45-foot outside wall, Cork Marcheschi's electric lines hung horizontally, emitting electric charges that touched off blue sparks and a rapid-fire artillery of sound. Inside, Sam Gilliam's large bolt of painted cloth was suspended from the ceiling, while Lynda Benglis' 10-unit polyurethane black foam piece jutted out from the wall. Making full use of the new space, Dan Flavin built a 74-foot tunnel, one end anchored over a stairway, and lit the ceiling with a grid of blue, cool pink, yellow, and green fluorescent lights.

<
Dan Flavin's installation *untitled (to Elizabeth and Richard Koshalek)*, created for the opening exhibition in the new building, 1971

■ The entire building is a virtuoso performance, on a site so small that one feels that no museum this size . . . could possibly have been fitted into the available space. . . . [The Walker is] beginning to shift the center of gravity of the American art world from New York to this rather intriguing little Midwestern city previously known chiefly for its production of perfect thermostats (*Architecture Plus*). ■

growth inside and out

Despite the economic uncertainty of the 1970s, the Walker continued to grow, selling off parts of its original nineteenth-century collection and continuing to expand its reach into the contemporary and avant-garde. Although films had been screened at the Walker since 1946, the Film/Video Department did not become "official" until 1973, when the Edmond R. Ruben Film and Video Study Collection was established. Visiting filmmakers became a major Walker attraction through such programs as the Regis Dialogue and Retrospective; participants have included Robert Altman, Jim Jarmusch, Jodie Foster, Hanif Kureishi, Jane Campion, Tom Hanks, Jessica Lange, and Spike Lee.

In 1976, the T. B. Walker Foundation gave the Walker $27 million, $10.5 million of which was an endowment, and the Walker Art Center became a public institution. It acquired the buildings housing the museum and theater, the land, and most of the collection, which then included nineteenth-century landscapes, modern European and American Expressionist works, and sculpture by Picasso, Calder, and Henry Moore.

By 1983, more than a decade after the Barnes building opened, the Walker was again desperate for space. Once more Barnes applied his minimalist logic, designing a new gallery below ground level on the Lyndale side, a 70-seat lecture room, a new print study room, an extended bookshop and art lab in which children's art classes were now being offered, and an addition on the south side that provided more office, shop, and storage space. The $5.2-million addition opened September 23, 1984, after 19 months of construction by Minneapolis firms Hammel, Green and Abrahamson, Inc. and M. A. Mortenson Company.

>
Sol LeWitt's design for the lower lobby of the new building, 1984

The latest expansion also launched the McKnight Print Study Room. In 1983, the Walker had acquired the Tyler Graphics Archive and by 1984 owned more than 1,000 prints, rare proofs, and one-of-a-kind-works on paper by various artists made in collaboration with New York master printer Kenneth Tyler. The opening exhibition, *Prints from Tyler Graphics*, featured work from artists such as Frank Stella, Helen Frankenthaler, Roy Lichtenstein, and David Hockney. A complete set of Jasper Johns prints joined the collection in 1988, and in 1990 an agreement was made with the artist that his print archive at the Walker would be kept up-to-date in perpetuity.

Barnes won an American Institute of Architects Award for "perhaps the finest building for the display of contemporary art built in the last generation," as the *New York Times* described it. But Barnes' work wasn't done. Friedman and the Walker Board of Directors had a bigger civic vision. Across Vineland Place stood a large, unoccupied bit of land in an area dubbed the Parade in 1904. Around the turn of the century, the Kenwood Armory, a large brick building used for shows, fights, and even a John Philip Sousa performance, was built on peat bogs and quicksand. Its poor foundation and subsequent cracking led to its demise in 1933, but the formal flower beds next to it, called the Armory Gardens, were deeded to the Minneapolis Park Board and maintained until 1966, when a freeway dissected the area. To Barnes, it seemed a perfect setting for a sculpture park.

^
The McKnight Print Study Room, built to house the Walker's print collection, 1984

>
The Kenwood Armory and adjacent gardens, circa 1915

^
The Minneapolis
Sculpture Garden, 1998

Twenty thousand people attended the Minneapolis Sculpture Garden's opening weekend on September 10 and 11, 1988. Barnes had designed a 7.5-acre, $12-million garden that blends formal and informal, temporary and permanent. Four roofless rooms, each 100-by-100 feet, are bordered by low granite walls and evergreen hedges that lead to a fifth giant room surrounded by evergreens. The Cowles Conservatory, which houses Frank Gehry's *Standing Glass Fish*, also graces the site.

<
View of the Minneapolis Sculpture Garden with the Cowles Conservatory in the foreground

>
Frank Gehry
Standing Glass Fish
(1986), wood, glass, steel, silicone, plexiglass and rubber
Gift of Anne Pierce Rogers in honor of her grandchildren, Anne and Will Rogers and Lily Rogers Grant, 1986

<
Installation of
Spoonbridge and Cherry
as the centerpiece of
the Minneapolis
Sculpture Garden, 1988

One sculpture highlight, commissioned by the Walker and destined to become an icon for Minneapolis itself, was Claes Oldenburg and Coosje van Bruggen's *Spoonbridge and Cherry.* A 1,200-pound cherry, 9.5 feet in diameter with water spraying out of its 12-foot stem, rests on a 52-foot spoon surrounded by a pond. (The whimsical work is one of several that emerged from Oldenburg's fascination with a novelty spoon, its bowl resting in a gob of fake chocolate, that he'd bought in 1962.)

>
Claes Oldenburg and Coosje van Bruggen
Spoonbridge and Cherry (1985–88), aluminum, stainless steel and paint
Gift of Frederick R. Weisman in honor of his parents, William and Mary Weisman, 1988

Another icon is the Irene Hixon Whitney Bridge, a 375-foot, steel-and-wood footbridge created by Siah Armajani to cross the 16 lanes of traffic that stream above and below ground along the Garden's edge. A poem by John Ashbery adorns the steel span.

When the Parade Stadium was torn down in 1990, another $2 million in donations provided four more acres for the Garden, and the expansion was designed by Massachusetts-based Michael Van Valkenburgh Associates, Inc. It has proved a popular site for performances, community celebrations, and weddings, not to mention the casual walks and talks of museum visitors, neighbors, and urban wanderers. In 2003 alone, 328,000 people dropped by.

^
Detail of John Ashbery's poem on the Irene Hixon Whitney Bridge

<
View of the Minneapolis Sculpture Garden with Siah Armajani's Irene Hixon Whitney Bridge in the background

>
The Merce Cunningham Dance Company performs at the Minneapolis Sculpture Garden's tenth-anniversary celebration, September 1998

twenty-first-century town square

The end of the decade marked the end of another era. T. B. Walker's beloved Hudson River paintings no longer reflected the Walker's mission; in 1989, after great deliberation, Board members granted Sotheby's permission to sell Frederic Edwin Church's 1852 *Home by the Lake* (*Scene in the Catskill Mountains*). It fetched $8.5 million, the most that had ever been paid for a nineteenth-century work. These funds established the first endowment for the acquisition of new art.

In 1994, the Walker received the largest program grant in its history: a five-year, $1.125-million "New Definitions/New Audiences" Museum Collections Accessibility Initiative grant from the Lila Wallace-Reader's Digest Fund. (The grant was renewed in 2000.) It was clear that the Walker had no intention of ceasing, or even slowing, its forward momentum in exploring the horizons of contemporary art for an increasingly diverse audience.

"The Walker is known for its singular dedication to sponsoring and nurturing new works," says Kathy Halbreich, who became director in 1991. "Commissions are a vital form of cultural research and development, providing artists the time, space, and resources to research, experiment, and develop."

>
Artist-in-residence Joanna Haigood's *Picture Powderhorn*, a commissioned dance performance incorporating sound and video projection on a grain silo in Minneapolis

Outreach was important, too. The Walker was not a single experience, its leaders contended; its goal was to be many things to many people, ideally people who represented all backgrounds, persuasions, neighborhoods, interests, needs, and sensibilities. Free First Saturdays, Free Thursdays, and Explore memberships expanded accessibility and drew the curious. In 1994, the Walker became the country's first museum to devote staff solely to creating programs for teens, via the Teen Arts Council. In 1999 and again in 2003, multiyear Bush Foundation grants funded a new global initiative, which allowed the Walker to continue to welcome such artists-in-residence as Rirkrit Tiravanija (Thailand) and Robin Rhode (South Africa), and to acquire the work of such artists as Lee Bul (Korea), Huang Yong Ping (China), and Rivane Neuenschwander (Brazil).

But it was time for that historic bugaboo—space—to reassert itself on the priority list. As the *Minneapolis Star* noted when the Barnes building first opened in 1971, some reservations were justified, even then.

^
A meeting of the Walker Art Center Teen Arts Council with artist-in-residence Robin Rhode in the Art Lab, 2003

›
Artist-in-residence Julie Mehretu and students from Edison High School in Minneapolis develop their project "Minneapolis and St. Paul Are East African Cities," 2003

■ The most serious have to do with location. The building site is closely hemmed in, and present construction covers it virtually completely. There will be no room to expand if the Walker should again outgrow itself, as it did between 1927 and 1968. There is also the problem that, where it is, the Center is surrounded by strangling roadways. Access, parking, and landscaping will all likely be somewhat unsatisfactory for the foreseeable future. ■

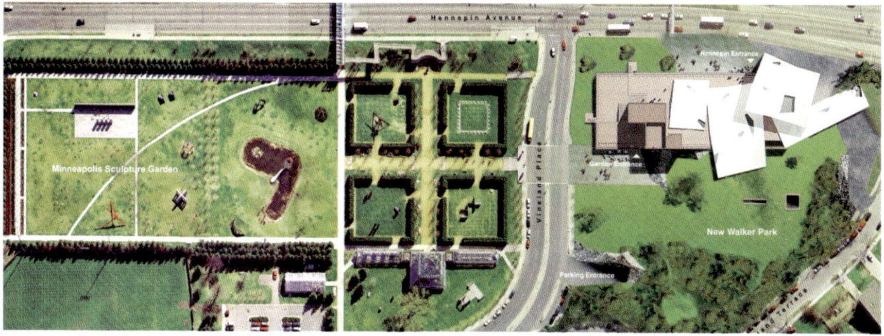

>
Site plan of the expanded Walker Art Center campus showing the new building addition in white at upper right

That future had arrived. Fortunately, a confluence of events offered an unforeseen opportunity. In 1945, the North American Life and Casualty Insurance Company had bought the Walker family home and built a large office building in its place. But after five decades, what was now Allianz Life Insurance had outgrown its quarters. In early 1999, the Walker used $11 million from its endowment to reclaim the site.

Meanwhile, the Guthrie Theater had been chafing in its cramped space. Although community activists clamored to preserve what had once been an important architectural icon, others argued that facelifts and redesigns had already rendered the once-distinctive Ralph Rapson structure a distant memory. Hungry for more room and rejuvenation, the Guthrie was exploring relocation plans along the Mississippi River near the old mill sites, where the riverfront was beginning to enjoy a long-anticipated cultural renaissance.

If the Guthrie moved, the Walker could stretch out, using luxurious new space to the west to add onto the compact Barnes cubes. Halbreich envisioned more of a gathering place than a museum, an expansive and open structure where people would convene to engage in debate and conversation. Diverse and lively, it would be a town square where visitors could experience all forms of art, "where ideas are the driving force."

^
Director Kathy Halbreich (far right foreground) reviews plans and materials for the new building with architects Jacques Herzog (center) and Christine Binswanger (far left)

<
Herzog & de Meuron, Goetz Collection, Gallery for a Private Collection of Modern Art, Munich, Germany, 1991–92

<
Herzog & de Meuron,
Tate Modern, London,
United Kingdom,
1998–2000

The Board encouraged Halbreich to conduct an extensive search involving some 35 candidates, which yielded Swiss architectural firm Herzog & de Meuron as creators of the next incarnation of the Walker Art Center. No strangers to the art world, Jacques Herzog and Pierre de Meuron had collaborated with Joseph Beuys on their first project: designing suits for 70 members of a marching band. Using materials in new and unexpected ways had long been their design forte.

Close friends since kindergarten, the pair studied together and launched their business in Basel in 1978. They were drawn to anonymous buildings; simple shapes and everyday materials became their themes. In the 1980s they designed houses and blocks of apartments, and they earned critical acclaim in 1992 for their design of the Goetz Collection, a private gallery in a Munich suburb. In 2001, they won the Pritzker Prize, architecture's Nobel, for work such as the conversion of London's Bankside Power Station into the Tate Modern, and Napa Valley's Dominus Winery, a long, low building constructed of gabions, metal cages filled with stones.

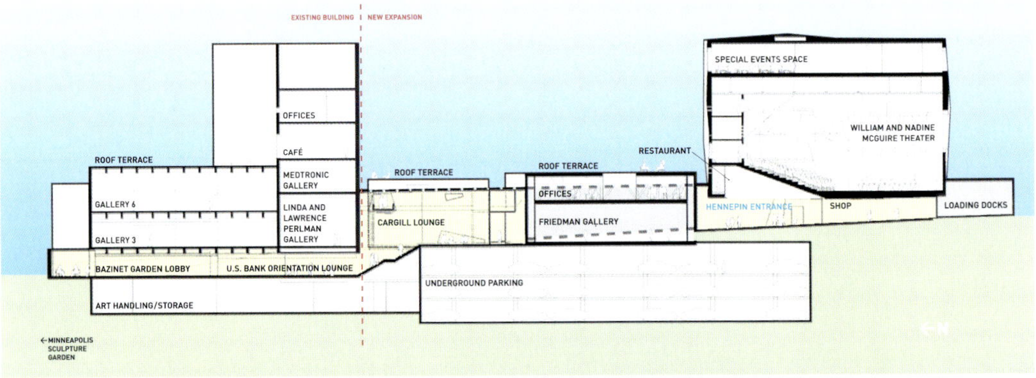

^
Walker Art Center expansion, section view from new garden

According to architect Jeffrey Kipnis, they were known primarily for "ceaselessly inventive architecture." In a conversation with Kipnis, Herzog explained why: "Nothing is more boring or stupid than to wake up in the morning naively confident in what you already know."

A tailor's son, Herzog is fascinated by the architect's version of clothing—building surfaces that act as skins, or veils, or, as author Naomi Stungo wrote in her 2002 book *Herzog and de Meuron*, "tantalizing, enticing gauze through which to glimpse, but not fully see, what's going on inside." The printed glass and concrete of the Eberswalde Library in Germany and the tower of concave and convex glass that comprises Tokyo's flagship Prada

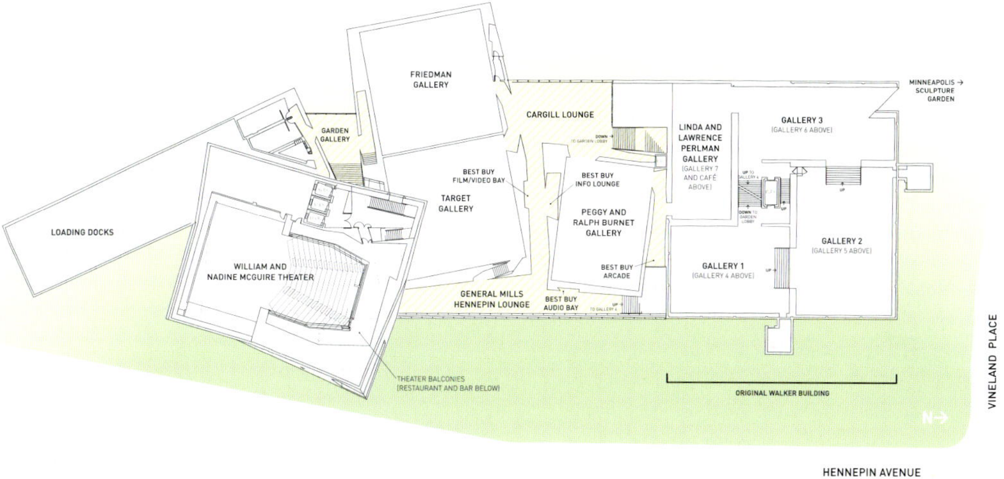

^

Walker Art Center expansion, floor plan with the William and Nadine McGuire Theater

store are examples of the innovative skill Herzog & de Meuron would need to marry the spare brick of the Barnes design to the open, welcoming town square now envisioned.

In 2002, with a flick of his wrist, Herzog presented his self-proclaimed "magic and sexy" design by flinging a handful of notepapers onto a table. "The overlapping sheets fanned out like a winning poker hand — which is roughly the configuration the expanded Walker will have when it opens in 2005" (*Star Tribune*). Hammel, Green and Abrahamson, Inc. were architects of record, M. A. Mortenson Company was the builder, and Christine Binswanger was the Herzog & de Meuron partner in charge of the project.

<
The mesh-paneled surface of the cube reflects the changing light, construction view

The loose collection of intersecting spaces, notable for its nod to transparency, is perhaps the antithesis of the stark, solid Barnes building; the two are connected by a glass link. Herzog had hoped to create a translucent white exterior for the new cube, lit from within like a paper lantern, but testing of the proposed Teflon fabric revealed a few flaws; for one, its evening glow would attract the state's overabundant mosquito population. Additionally, the stretch of the fabric around the building's edges would resemble a poorly wrapped birthday present. Instead, the surface is clad in aluminum mesh panels embossed with an irregular pattern of creases that catch natural light and reflect the ever-changing weather. Looking rather like the surface of a frozen lake, the structure suggests a fragility that softens the effect of its mass; it is cantilevered over the plaza below, offering diners in the restaurant a dramatic view of the avenue.

>
The glass curtain wall of the General Mills Hennepin Lounge leads to the cantilevered restaurant and the entrance along Hennepin Avenue, construction view

>
The floor of the General Mills Hennepin Lounge mimics the brick on the Barnes building, connecting it to the expansion, construction view

The building is multifaceted, with unique sides and exterior gallery walls that fold and cant in dynamic trajectories. Its floor echoes the familiar Barnes brick. Asymmetric windows punctuate the facade, revealing inside activity and connecting art-browsers to street life. Inner and outer lighting designed by Arnold Chan, founder of London's Isometrix Lighting + Design, creates a soft, luminous evening presence.

On its now 17-acre campus, the $67.5-million expansion adds 130,000 square feet, nearly doubling the Walker's size. In the past decade, the Walker collection had grown 40 percent, yet less than two percent could be displayed at once. The 11 galleries increase exhibition space from 30,000 to 40,000 square feet; visitors will see more work by artists such as Joseph Beuys, Bruce Conner, Agnes Martin, Donald Judd, and Sigmar Polke. The new galleries, still minimalist white, show off the physicality of the building. Their large size allows them to house such shows as those celebrating the 2005 reopening: one featuring Robert Motherwell, Jasper Johns, Ellsworth Kelly, and Joan Mitchell; and another presenting a newer generation of equally influential artists—Kara Walker, Matthew Barney, Robert Gober, and Sherrie Levine.

Just as the Walker integrates artistic disciplines, its design physically interweaves galleries with event spaces and informal lounges. Interstitial spaces between galleries feature interactive educational activities. Amenities include a full-service restaurant and café and an underground parking garage. The state-of-the art, 385-seat William and Nadine McGuire Theater will accommodate those who come to watch more than 70 contemporary dance, music, and theater performances a year. Its expansive stage size, combined with its intimate setting, offer a rare public venue for developing performances on-site and engaging visitors in the creative process.

v
The auto court, an entrance to the underground parking garage, Walker Art Center expansion

>
The patterned ceiling and entrance door of the Target Gallery allow visitors a glimpse of the exhibition after hours

^
The new special events space offers a spectacular view of the city skyline

T. B. Walker's open-house concept has returned. A new entrance on the well-traveled Hennepin Avenue beckons visitors while yielding dramatic downtown skyline views from 20-foot-high windows running parallel to the street. Inside, visitors can pause at the Best Buy Audio and Film/Video bays or explore the Best Buy Info Lounge, where the media table *Dialog* recognizes hand gestures and makes interactivity a social experience.

<
The passageway to the Cargill Lounge connects the city with the garden

Leaving behind the east-side city bustle, the western entrance opens onto a new four-acre park, a respectful neighbor to the residences beyond and casual mate to the more formal sculpture garden. Known for his innovative European plazas combining lush plantings and crisp geometric spaces, French landscape architect Michel Desvigne has fashioned a blend of birch and aspen trees, bluestem prairie-grass meadows, and mowed lawn for picnics. The Cargill Lounge, with its glass outer walls, provides a gentle transition from inside to outdoors.

>
Prototype of *Dialog*, an interactive table designed by Marek Walczak, Jakub Segen, Michael McAllister, and Peter Kennard

Artist James Turrell, who spent years shaping an extinct northern Arizona volcano crater into a bowl of natural light, was commissioned to create a *Skyspace* for the new garden. From the park, it looks like a minimalist cube that is reminiscent of the Barnes wing in miniature. Inside the 23-square-foot underground room, as many as 30 people can view the ever-changing sky through an 11-square-foot opening.

The convergence of green space and cityscape, bright glass interior streets and dark brick boxes, galleries for quiet contemplation and lounges for active conversation is a fitting scene for the latest chapter in the Walker's history. Not unlike T. B. Walker's early notion of a terrace that assembled books and art for perusal by the public, the newest design also speaks of converging disciplines: visual arts, not just painting, sculpture, and design; performing arts, not just dance, music, and theater; and media arts, not just film, video, and digital art. All of these require space that is as flexible and adaptable as the contemporary arts and as visionary as the artists themselves.

■ Just as T. B. Walker refused to relegate his collection to an isolate room, "this nonhierarchical grouping of disciplines can't be contained in silolike traditional museums," Halbreich says. "We have a holistic view, and we've worked hard to develop and encourage crossover opportunities. The multidisciplinary convergence that began in the 1970s was critical in leveling the traditional hierarchies, and in making it possible to engage with art in its myriad variations in a town square setting. That's why it's a center, as opposed to a museum." It's also why the Walker, true to its legacy, continues to be a unique venue for the arts of its time. ■

>
Rendering of the new Walker Art Center, view along Hennepin Avenue

WALKER ART CENTER
PICTURE SHOW

The Walker Art Center gratefully acknowledges the contributions of design director Andrew Blauvelt, associate editor Pamela Johnson, slide librarian Stephanie Kays, editor Kathleen McLean, publications manager Lisa Middag, and archivist Jill Vetter for their able assistance on this book.

Walker Art Center
1750 Hennepin Avenue
Minneapolis, Minnesota 55403
USA

walkerart.org

First published in 2005 by
Scala Publishers Limited
Northburgh House
10 Northburgh Street
London EC1V OAT
United Kingdom

Distributed outside the Walker Art Center
to the book trade by
Antique Collectors' Club Limited
Eastworks
116 Pleasant Street, Suite 60B
Easthampton, MA 01027
United States of America

ISBN: 1 85759 377 4

Text by Cathy Madison
Designed by Janet James
Produced by Scala Publishers
Printed and bound by Everbest, China.

Photography credits:

Tom Arndt, p. 25; Edward Larrabee Barnes, p. 29 (top); Studios of Camera Craft, Minneapolis, p. 13 (right); Rolphe Dauphin, pp. 14, 16 (left and bottom right), 18 (left), 20, 21; Clark Dean, p. 23 (left); Dan Dennehy, pp. 45, 47; Glenn Halvorson, pp. 3, 37, 38, 40, 42, 44; © 2004 Herzog & de Meuron, pp. 49, 52, 53, 62–63; *Minneapolis Times*, p. 18 (right); *Minneapolis Tribune*, p. 27 (right); The Minnesota Historical Society, p. 39; Pathé News, p. 12; Gene Pittman, front cover, p. 54; © 1999–2004 Margherita Spiluttini, all rights reserved, pp. 50 (bottom), 51; Ezra Stoller © Esto, p. 22; Eric Sutherland, back cover, pp. 1, 16 (top right), 24, 26, 27 (left), 29 (bottom), 30, 31, 32, 33, 34, 35; Walker Art Center Archives, pp. 5, 6, 7, 8, 9, 11, 13 (left), 23 (right); Cameron Wittig, pp. 4, 48, 50 (top), 55, 57, 58, 59, 60, 61.